Single and Lonely

Finding the Intimacy You Desire

Jayne V. Clark

New
Growth
Press
www.newgrowthpress.com

New Growth Press, Greensboro, NC 27429
Copyright © 2009 by Jayne V. Clark
All rights reserved. Published 2009.

Typesetting: Robin Black, www.blackbirdcreative.biz

ISBN-10: 1-934885-99-1
ISBN-13: 978-1-934885-99-4

Library of Congress Cataloging-in-Publication Data

Clark, Jayne V., 1956-
  Single and lonely : finding the intimacy you desire / Jayne V. Clark.
    p. cm.
  Includes bibliographical references and index.
  ISBN-13: 978-1-934885-99-4 (alk. paper)
  ISBN-10: 1-934885-99-1 (alk. paper)
  1. Loneliness—Religious aspects—Christianity. 2. Single people—Religious life. I. Title.
  BV4911.C37 2009
  248.8′6—dc22

                                    2009014709

Printed in Canada

11 12 13   4 5 6

erhaps you are single by choice—you want to be on your own for a while, enjoying the freedom and benefits of adulthood. Perhaps it's not your choice, and a divorce, death, or broken relationship has propelled you back into singleness. Or maybe the opportunity for a serious relationship has never arisen. But whatever your situation, sometimes you feel lonely and long for companionship. It's natural to desire someone with whom you can share your life, and it's easy to think, *If I were married or just had some kind of relationship, then I wouldn't be lonely.* But will a change in your circumstances really solve your problem with loneliness?

A Common Experience

Unfortunately, getting married won't protect you from loneliness; married people get lonely too. Sometimes it's because the marriage isn't all that great. Maybe the only thing they share is the same bed. Maybe the only thing they agree on is to avoid talking to one another. Whatever the reasons, the reality is that marriage has fallen far short of their dreams. They are lonelier now than they've ever been.

Even spouses in great marriages sometimes feel lonely. A young couple splits their days between work and classes, studying all night and spending their weekends serving at church. A mother struggles when her husband is away on business trips, while he spends his evenings in lonely hotel rooms. A man who has worked his entire life so he and his wife can spend their retirement traveling together now spends every moment caring for her as she slips away with Alzheimer's. He's committed to her, but he's lonely.

The list of people who experience loneliness goes on and on. People change jobs and move away from family and friends. The elderly spend hours alone in nursing homes. An alcoholic finds himself living on the streets. Soldiers serving overseas miss their families. Kids go off to college. Prisoners are in isolation. Patients are confined to bed. The list includes the person living next to you. It includes you—but *not* just because you are single. All of us, at one time or another, experience loneliness.

Circumstances vary, but the feelings are similar. We feel isolated, vulnerable, and alone. We want to talk and be heard. We want to be known and understood; we don't want to feel invisible. We want to be included and cared about. We desire intimacy. We want to be connected to someone.

A Flawed Strategy

So how do we remedy this loneliness? When I was a child I thought it was simple: Make one really good friend. I was a good listener, and I combined that with a decent sense of humor and a willingness to be helpful. My job was to listen, make you laugh, and help you out. Your job was to be my friend so I wouldn't be lonely. But eventually I would upset the balance of this arrangement by asking you to help me. If you couldn't manage it, I felt hurt. Or maybe I couldn't get you to listen to me for ten minutes when I had already listened to you for hours. In either case, I wouldn't dare tell you that I was hurt because you might have gotten upset with me. So I would take self-protective steps to prevent getting hurt again.

Do you see the dynamic? I work to get you to like me, but I also work to protect myself from you. I move toward you because I want your acceptance, but I back away because I want to play it safe. A tug-of-war goes on within my heart. My desire for acceptance wins one moment, self-protection the next. The result? I send out a continuous stream of mixed messages. When I am self-protective, I withdraw into myself. But then I become afraid you are (a) losing patience with me; (b) glad to be rid of me; or (c) not even noticing that I've withdrawn. All of these possibilities are bad, so I risk getting hurt by being nice again so you'll still like me. Sooner or later, it all takes too much effort, and we drift apart. But eventually, loneliness gets to me, the memories fade, and I begin the cycle all over again with someone else.

I didn't always realize that my strategies not only increased my own loneliness, but added to other people's loneliness as well. Neither did I realize what was going on in me beneath the surface. At a very basic level I was treating my friends like objects, manipulating them so they would do what I wanted. When they let me down, I saw them as obstacles to my sense of security and belonging.

The Remedy for Loneliness

In his mercy, God didn't leave me to endlessly repeat this cycle. He opened my eyes to this reality: it isn't what remedies our loneliness, but who remedies it—namely, Jesus Christ, the friend of sinners.

Loneliness is a result of man's original sin against God in the Garden of Eden (Genesis 3:1–13). The perfect union Adam and Eve had enjoyed with God and with each other was destroyed when they chose to disobey God. Sin separated them from God and from each other. Where once there had been openness (they had been naked and unashamed), sin made for hiding (behind fig leaves and trees). Where once there had been completeness, sin made for loss. Where once there had been acceptance, sin made for rejection. Where once there had been praise, sin made for blame ("she made me do it"). Hiding. Loss. Rejection. Blame. All ingredients of loneliness. Loneliness was born at the Fall.

It is true that before sin entered the world, God had declared that it wasn't good for man to be alone (Genesis 2:18), but God was stating a fact, not voicing how Adam was feeling. At the time, Adam was enjoying perfect communion with God. Apart from God telling him, he had no way of knowing that anything more was possible. Maybe Adam began to get an inkling of it as the animals paraded past him, but it was God's assessment that man should not be alone. This shouldn't surprise us. After all, God created man in his image, and he is not a God who exists alone. He is one God in three persons—three who are alike, yet distinct. God wanted man to enjoy fellowship with him, but he also wanted man to enjoy the kind of fellowship God enjoys as three members of the Godhead—with others who are like us, but distinct from us. Because we are made in God's image, we are made to be in relationship with him *and* with other people.

Some have implied, if not stated outright, that marriage is the solution to loneliness. But where would that leave a child who won't have that option for years? Or a prisoner with no hope of parole? Or an elderly widow or widower? This notion suggests that one category of people is potentially exempt from loneliness, and the rest of us are just stuck with it. But that's not true. Remember, it was *a married couple* who first experienced loneliness. And consider this: if marriage was God's answer to loneliness, why won't there be marriage in heaven? That's kind of a trick question because actually there will be. Only it won't be individuals who are married in heaven. It will be God's people corporately—the church, the bride of Christ—who will finally meet the bridegroom Jesus face to face (Revelation 19:1–9).

The real solution to loneliness lies not in marriage, but in our union with Christ, which leads to our union with one another. When God created Eve, he created marriage; but more than that, he created community.

Marriage is a form of community, perhaps its most basic and elemental form. Community requires people coming together. In marriage it happens literally. Community usually involves the group expanding. In marriage this happens by bearing children. But God's plans are always bigger and better than ours.

When God called Abram to follow him, he told him that his descendants would outnumber the grains of sand on the seashore and that all the nations of the earth would be blessed through him (Genesis 12:1–3; 13:16). God always had in mind a community made up of those from every tribe and language and people and nation. But the Israelites, Abram's descendants, were so caught up in being the chosen race that they overlooked that part.

Even today we're not much different. We're big on family, but we tend to think of it narrowly—as in our own personal, nuclear families. Yet when Jesus was told that his mother and brothers wanted to speak to him, he said, "Who is my mother, and who are my brothers? . . . Whoever does the will of my Father in heaven is my brother and sister and mother" (Matthew 12:48, 50). Jesus was redefining and enlarging the meaning of family. It's still based on blood—but it's his shed blood.

When you look at Genesis 2 through the lens of Jesus' work on the cross, you will be blown away. Yes, it's wonderful that a husband and wife become one flesh; but it's even more wonderful that Christians comprise the body of Christ, so connected with each other that if one part suffers, we all suffer. If one part is honored, we are all honored. It's incredible for a husband and wife to come together, to be fruitful and multiply; but it's even more incredible that Christ grows and multiplies his kingdom by sending flawed people like us to "go and make disciples of all nations" (Matthew 28:19). It must have been fantastic for Adam and Eve to be naked yet unashamed with each other; but it's even more fantastic that Jesus has washed away our sin, and we now stand clothed in his righteousness! We don't need to hide behind fig leaves when our sin is exposed. Now we can confess our sins to one another.

This is what Jesus has done for us. He went to the cross, betrayed and deserted by his friends. As he hung there, becoming saturated with our sin, even his Father had to turn away from him. Has there ever been a lonelier moment? Adam and Eve hid among the trees because of their sin, but Jesus hung naked and exposed on a tree because of our sin. Adam and Eve were guilty, yet tried to pass the blame. Jesus was completely innocent, yet he took our blame on himself. Jesus was rejected by his Father so we could be accepted. He gave up everything so God might lavish his blessings on us. Because of Jesus' love for his Father—and their love for us—Jesus hung on the cross until he died. By paying the penalty for our sin, he reversed the effects of the Fall and turned the tide on loneliness.

Loneliness Can Be Relieved

Do the effects of sin still linger? Of course. Loneliness will not be eliminated until we get to heaven. But in Jesus Christ and through his work, change is possible. Loneliness can be eased for us and by us. When I tried to handle it on my own, I did not understand that I needed to love people rather than fear them or use them. Through my counseling classes and Ed Welch's book, *When People Are Big and God Is Small*, God helped me to identify what was going on in my heart and repent of it.

Have I arrived? Certainly not. Ask anyone who knows me. But now, at least, I know to pray, "Search me, O God, and know my heart; test me and know my anxious thoughts. See if there is any offensive way in me, and lead me in the way everlasting" (Psalm 139:23–24).

I encourage you to ask the Lord to show you where you intensify your own loneliness and, even more importantly, the loneliness of others. For instance, some of us consider ourselves introverted or shy. To us, there's nothing more intimidating than starting a conversation. What a great opportunity for a heart check! Ask yourself what's holding you back. Fear of rejection? Fear of being embarrassed? You may be surprised to discover that it's actually pride: You don't want anyone to discover your flaws. Or maybe you don't want to be seen talking to someone "like that." There are lots of possibilities. Ask God to show you.

Maybe you are extroverted and outgoing. It is easy for you to talk to people you've never met before. In fact, you talk and talk and no one else can get a word in edgewise! What's going on? Pride? Do you love to impress people with how smart or funny you are? Or perhaps it's fear. You're afraid of silence or of being alone. Ask God to show you.

Whatever you might find when God shows you your heart, remember that God wants to change you—and me—to make us more like him, more like the people he created us to be. When we surrender ourselves to him and let him work in us, amazing things happen. First, our relationship with him deepens. We find ourselves actually relating to him rather than just referring to our relationship with him. That kind of change certainly reduces our loneliness.

Changed Priorities and Perspectives

God also changes our priorities. Rather than being self-absorbed, we become more focused on others. If your goal is to solve your loneliness, you will end up using people as I did. But when you "seek first the kingdom of God and his righteousness" (Matthew 6:33, ESV) you will end up loving people. Along the way you'll discover that you're just not as lonely as you used to be. In fact, you may find you're not lonely at all.

How might these changed priorities play out in your life? It might mean that you notice the aloneness of others—and instead of waiting for an invitation you invite a single-parent family over for dinner. It could mean reaching out to an elderly couple and helping them with the more strenuous household chores. Or perhaps you could run your errands with someone else. We all have errands to run, so why not make it a social occasion?

You may be thinking, *I'm too busy as it is. I don't have time for that!* But when you take these kinds of steps, relationships develop. Your perspective changes and you find that certain activities don't seem as important as they used to. You may also find many times that double benefits occur. Having a family over for dinner gives you the opportunity to have fun with the kids, which also gives their parent a break. As you help the elderly couple with household chores, they share with you the wisdom of their years. When you run errands with someone else, you wind up helping each other with other mundane tasks, and that makes them easier and more enjoyable for both of you.

What are some other ways to move toward people? Let's take a look at three:

1. Look and see.

How many people cross our paths every day? Shop clerks, bank tellers, trash collectors, neighbors, people we pass on the street, or those who sit behind us in church services week after week. All these people blend into the background of our busy lives. We give them a nod, but that's it. Have we looked at them and seen them as people God has put in our paths to love, even in the simplest ways?

God sees us and watches over us. Remember Hagar in Genesis 16? Sarah could not conceive Abraham's child, so she decided that Hagar her maidservant should bear Abraham a son. When Hagar conceived and Ishmael was born, Hagar treated Sarah with contempt. Sarah reacted by driving Hagar into the desert. Surprisingly, the angel of the Lord followed Hagar and spoke with her. Hagar was amazed! She said, "You are the God who sees me" (Genesis 16:13). Hagar, a slave woman, was not invisible to God. Should anyone now be "invisible" to us?

In Luke 7 Jesus was on his way to the town of Nain with his disciples. A large crowd followed them. Amid all the activity, Jesus saw a grieving mother and his heart went out to her. He stopped to comfort her and restored her dead son back to life. The Gospels are filled with accounts of Jesus seeing hungry, lost, hurting people and reaching out to meet their needs. How are we going to minister to a world full of lonely people if we haven't first looked to see them?

2. Listen.

Something else we can do to move toward people is to listen to them—listen well. We serve a God who knows our every thought. He knows our words before they even reach our tongues, yet he encourages us to talk to him. When we do, he listens. Why? Because he wants us to relate to him, as a child to his father. How do we know he listens? Because Scripture records conversations he had with people—conversations that included give-and-take dialog between God and Abraham, Moses, Job, and many others. The Lord of the universe listens to us too.

If God cares enough to listen to us, how can we not care enough to listen to others? Listen not only to the words they say, but listen also for what they mean. Notice what their tone of voice, facial expressions, and body language are communicating. Listening well requires us to take a genuine interest in others. It also requires patience and wisdom that come only by the work of God's Spirit in us.

3. Touch.

Touch can ease the loneliness of others. This is a sensitive subject since we live in a society where practically everything has been sexualized. Even Christians are prone to read all kinds of things into innocent actions. I'm not naïve; I know that sinful touching occurs even within the church. However, the correct response is not to avoid touching or to be paralyzed by fear of lawsuits. Rather, the church should be a place where we treat one another as family members with "absolute purity" (1 Timothy 5:1–2).

Jesus didn't just talk to the people he healed. He touched them, and he let them touch him, too. Those who have been physically or sexually abused should be able to find comfort and healing not only in the words they hear at church, but also in the touch they receive—touch that conveys nothing more or less than kindness. Do we want to be sensitive to people's experiences and wise in the way we go about it? Absolutely! But we don't want to overcompensate by never reaching out with a touch at all. When someone has been deprived of touch or hurt by inappropriate touch, it is wonderful to see her respond with joy when she is touched in kindness with the love of Christ.

Scripture tells us to love one another (John 13:34). Next in line on the "one another" list is "greet one another with a holy kiss" (Romans 16:16). If that's a little too much for you, how about offering a handshake, a pat on the back, a touch on the forearm, or maybe a hug? God created us with skin that is sensitive to touch, and he declared everything he created to be good. We, as the body of Christ, can offer his touch to lonely, hurting people.

A Community of Oneness with Christ

These suggestions are ways we can individually image Christ in a lonely world. But what can happen when people as a group decide to live out their oneness with Christ and each other? I once belonged to a church where the leadership didn't want to just *profess* that Christ was head of the Church; they wanted to *practice* it. They reasoned that Christ wouldn't lead some of them one way and the rest another, any more than we would tell one leg to walk right and the other left. They believed that he would lead them all in the same direction, so they agreed to submit first to Christ and then to each other. That meant decisions had to be unanimous, not decided by majority or consensus. And unanimity meant that everyone truly believed in and agreed upon the direction God was leading them. This is radical oneness.

One of the first things that needed to change was the way the church leadership conducted their meetings. Rather than opening with a brief devotional and prayer for the congregation, they began studying the Bible together and praying for themselves, repenting of their sins, and interceding for each other. Then they prayed for the congregation. Many were gifted businessmen who knew how to argue their positions and get their way, but this was a "whole new ball game." They had to die to themselves and their agendas to seek the mind of Christ. They had to really listen to each other, not just wait until someone stopped talking so they could speak their piece. God trained them in patience, humility, and forbearance with one another. They learned to appreciate each other's God-given gifts and perspectives. They developed a deep affection and respect for each other. They had begun by agreeing to a philosophy of ministry, but God knit their hearts together in love as they sought the mind of Christ.

At times there would be one or two who thought things should go one way, while the rest felt otherwise. They would pray and wait until they were all of one mind. Sometimes the many ended up agreeing with the few. At other times the few eventually agreed with the many. But rather than being frustrated by the process, thinking, *We've wasted so much time. Why couldn't you have agreed with us in the first place?* the leadership recognized that the delay was actually God's mercy to them. He had prevented them from moving ahead prematurely.

Sometimes the process was slow and painful. But something astounding happened! They not only learned to act as one, they also became one. The Holy Spirit enabled them to live out of their union with him to a degree they never had before. Their hearts were exposed and changed. They related to one another in new ways. Do you see the progression? Change in individual hearts led to change within the leadership, which then spread out into the congregation itself. God was growing and strengthening the church in a way that was faster and better than anything they could have done by their human efforts.

It didn't end there. Transformed members of the congregation reached into their neighborhoods, touching lives like never before. Those outside the church noticed and responded to the invitations of their neighbors. Others just showed up at church out of curiosity. In time, the makeover within the congregation resulted in a change in the makeup of the congregation. Men wearing Brooks Brothers' suits sat shoulder to shoulder with people in tee shirts and jeans.

Obviously, everyone involved was still only a sinner

saved by God's grace. Problems continued to arise that needed addressing. But nothing diminished the joy of witnessing firsthand an incredible answer to Jesus' prayer in John 17:20–23:

> My prayer is not for them alone. I pray also
> for those who will believe in me through their
> message, that all of them may be one, Father,
> just as you are in me and I am in you. May they
> also be in us so that the world may believe that
> you have sent me....I in them and you in me.
> May they be brought to complete unity to let
> the world know that you sent me and have loved
> them even as you have loved me.

Whether we are single or married, we will experience loneliness in this fallen world. But God wants to enter into our loneliness and transform it. He unites us to himself and each other in Jesus as we submit our lives to him; and he calls us to enter into the loneliness of those around us. I look forward to the day when we will be delivered completely from loneliness to oneness in him.

If you were helped by reading this booklet, perhaps you or someone you know would also be encouraged by these booklets:

Angry Children: Understanding and Helping Your Child Regain Control, Michael R. Emlet, M.Div., M.D.

Conflict: A Redemptive Opportunity, Timothy S. Lane, M.Div., D.Min.

Divorce Recovery: Growing and Healing God's Way, Winston T. Smith, M.Div.

Eating Disorders: The Quest for Thinness, Edward T. Welch, M.Div., Ph.D.

Facing Death with Hope: Living for What Lasts, David Powlison, M.Div., Ph.D.

Family Feuds: How to Respond, Timothy S. Lane, M.Div., D.Min.

Freedom from Guilt: Finding Release from Your Burdens, Timothy S. Lane, M.Div., D.Min.

Forgiving Others: Joining Wisdom and Love, Timothy S. Lane, M.Div., D.Min.

Healing after Abortion: God's Mercy Is for You, David Powlison, M.Div., Ph.D.

Help for Stepfamilies: Avoiding the Pitfalls and Learning to Love, Winston T. Smith, M.Div.

Help for the Caregiver: Facing the Challenges with Understanding and Strength, Michael R. Emlet, M.Div., M.D.

Help! My Spouse Committed Adultery: First Steps for Dealing with Betrayal, Winston T. Smith, M.Div.

Helping Your Adopted Child: Understanding Your Child's Unique Identity, Paul David Tripp, M.Div., D.Min.

How Do I Stop Losing It with My Kids? Getting to the Heart of Your Discipline Problems, William P. Smith, M.Div., Ph.D.

How to Love Difficult People: Receiving and Sharing God's Mercy, William P. Smith, M.Div., Ph.D.

It's All About Me: The Problem with Masturbation, Winston T. Smith, M.Div.

Living with an Angry Spouse: Help for Victims of Abuse, Edward T. Welch, M.Div., Ph.D.

Peer Pressure: Recognizing the Warning Signs and Giving New Direction, Paul David Tripp, M.Div., D.Min.

Recovering from Child Abuse: Healing and Hope for Victims, David Powlison, M.Div., Ph.D.

Renewing Marital Intimacy: Closing the Gap Between You and Your Spouse, David Powlison, M.Div., Ph.D.

Restoring Your Broken Marriage: Healing after Adultery, Robert D. Jones, M.Div., D.Min.

Should We Get Married? How to Evaluate Your Relationship, William P. Smith, M.Div., Ph.D.

Single Parents: Daily Grace for the Hardest Job, Robert D. Jones, M.Div., D.Min.

When Bad Things Happen: Thoughtful Answers to Hard Questions, William P. Smith, M.Div., Ph.D.

When the Money Runs Out: Hope and Help for the Financially Stressed, James C. Petty, M.Div., D.Min.

Who Does the Dishes? Decision Making in Marriage, Winston T. Smith, M.Div.

To learn more about CCEF, visit our website at www.ccef.org